VICTORIAN & EDWARDIAN BOATING

from old photographs

VICTORIAN & EDWARDIAN BOATING

from old photographs

Neil Wigglesworth

B. T. BATSFORD LTD
LONDON

© Neil Wigglesworth 1987
First published 1987

ISBN 0 7134 5510 1

Printed in Great Britain
by Anchor Brendon Ltd,
Tiptree, Essex
for the publishers,
B. T. Batsford Ltd
4 Fitzhardinge Street
London
W1H 0AH

INTRODUCTION

Boating, like most forms of Victorian and Edwardian culture, was flamboyant, naive, sublime, pretentious and often positively eccentric. Its story reflects the diversity of society from the noblest Lord to the humblest worker, faithfully showing evolutionary trends throughout seven of the most formative decades in British history. To do justice to this diversity one must look at the whole range of water-borne craft used during this period – that is boats used for work, pleasure and competition – learning how cultural and technical trends affected their employment.

Variety of boats

The range and number of craft is bewildering, containing every gradation from coracle to steam launch each fulfilling a specific purpose. To simplify one can categorize them into boats which were rowed, sailed, punted, paddled or under steam and, for good measure, add a sixth category for those craft which defy precise definition. Under rowing boats we find State barges, Thames lighters, ferryboats, racing eights, fours, pairs and sculls, skiffs, wherries, whiffs, randans, funnies, hoys, pilot gigs, Admiralty cutters, lifeboats, peter boats, dinghies and ordinary working boats sculled with a single stern oar. Sailing boats include Severn trows, Thames barges, cobles, luggers, ketches, schooners, yawls and cutters along with the variety of competition class yachts. Punting has houseboats, college barges, pontoons, a whole range of working punts, pleasure, touring and racing punts, whilst paddling includes Canadian canoes, Rob Roy canoes and kayaks. The steam category is simple in comparison, with paddle steamers, steam yachts, tugboats and narrow boats whereas the eccentric section would have to include such unusual types as coracles, dongolas, octuple scullers, gondolas and water cycles.

Historical background

Whether we take Dr. Johnson's definition of boating as 'impelling a vessel in water by oars' or that of an Edwardian author who extolled it as 'the most aristocratic and scientific of sports' we should realize that neither tells the full story. In 1454 John Norman, then Lord Mayor of London, commandeered a working Thames barge and decorated it for his procession to Westminster; the other City companies followed his example and a succession of Royal barges, propelled by up to 40 oarsmen, has enlivened the Thames scene ever since (fig. 6). Originally man power, supplemented occasionally by the wind, was the only method of propulsion, although where possible horses were placed in harness to haul the larger craft. The ancient Watermen's Company, which was restricted to River Thames workers on the stretch between Gravesend and Windsor, had exclusive control of all craft on the River Thames from Teddington to Gravesend and before the advent of steam had some 10,000 men under licence; if one considers the entire river and the whole range of water-borne trades there was a total of 100,000 men employed. The River Thames, although important, was by no means the only significant waterway and if one includes the coasts, inland lakes and canals it is apparent that the skills of the boatman were vital to the welfare of the nation. This state of affairs existed until technical developments made obsolete the old style craft and those who manned them, developments which had their first effects at the beginning of the Victorian era; the age of steam had begun. The first of the paddle steamers appeared on the River Clyde in 1812 and by 1837 they were commonplace. Together with the erection of more bridges over the Thames these paddle steamers were responsible for the virtual eradication of the London watermen by the end of the century. Water-borne trade was, at the same time, hit hard by the huge extension of the nationwide railway system and by 1880 the majority of cargoes formerly carried by the old sailing barges was travelling by road. In the first year of the new Queen's reign Charles Hulbert, a topographer from Shrewsbury, stood on Coalport bridge across the River Severn and counted 72 vessels below him, marvelling that 'this must be the most extraordinary district in the world'; only 40-odd years later the last barge was plying the local china trade. The rate of change was alarming and had national effects on employment: fishing fleets were rationalised, thousands of ferrymen made redundant, lightermen and dockers laid off and passenger carriers reduced to taking on second and even third jobs to make ends meet. The old wooden ships were superseded by iron craft and even then the adage ran that 'before, we had wooden ships and iron men but now we have iron ships and wooden men'!

Working boats

Some aquatic trades and skills such as gig rowing and coracle fishing lasted longer than others, and some craft remained virtually unchanged throughout the era. Perhaps the biggest popular newspaper story of 1838 was the rescue by Grace Darling of nine survivors from the *Forfarshire*, wrecked on the Farne Islands en route for Dundee; ironically the *Forfarshire* was one of the new paddle steamers and Grace and her father were entirely reliant upon their own strength in rowing an ancient Northumberland coble. The news of such heroism served as a boost to the fortunes of the Royal National Lifeboat Institution which had been formed in 1824, and by 1850 it was firmly established and promoting competitions to find the most suitable design for a life-saving vessel. One such design was built by the Richardson family of Lake Bala in North Wales in 1852 and rowed all the way from Liverpool to London to prove that it was seaworthy. Despite the resulting publicity, however, the tubular construction of the 40 foot boat never caught on. Most of the early boats were 12 oared craft of traditional design because the National Lifeboat Committee believed that rowing was the most important factor for getting off the beach in bad weather and the crews of local fishermen were far more confident in familiar craft (*fig. 22*). These early crewmen were highly paid for their work and would receive £1 an outing and almost as much for a practice session when a normal weekly wage was £3. These pulling boats were still in regular use until recently – the Whitby station only dispensed with theirs in 1957.

Other, smaller working boats retained their usefulness, like those employed for whammeling (fishing for salmon using a whammel net) in Morecambe Bay (*fig. 8*) and the Thames fishing punts of Chertsey, Staines and Windsor. The best survivor, however, was the coracle (*fig. 96*). This strange and ancient craft was particularly common on the River Severn around Ironbridge where the

Rogers family made them for a variety of uses. Ostensibly, the main use was cheap personal transport for the local factory workers who could then avoid the daily bridge tolls. Many of them were used, however, for poaching the rabbits from the otherwise inaccessible fields and copses of the river banks, and fishing forbidden stretches of the stream despite the knowledge that detection would result in severe punishment. Such punishments failed to deter men prompted by poverty and desperate need, as many were during Victoria's reign, and the little coracle was a swift and silent ally in their night-time exploits.

The advent of competition

For many working boats employed in traditional activities the element of competition was an integral and vital part of their role. The speed with which a Thames waterman delivered his passenger determined his income and led to unofficial sculling races. In turn, these became organized matches patronized by the nobility and watched by thousands. A contemporary sporting book lists some 5000 such matches in the years 1835 to 1851, which indicates a rate of five a week every week for 16 years. Other parts of the country were similarly affected and areas as diverse as Walney Channel in Cumbria, King's Lynn in Norfolk and Southampton Water saw professional sculling and rowing contests for thousands of pounds and, ultimately, the World Championships. Nowhere was more involved in aquatics than Newcastle-on-Tyne where the tradition of boating had been established by the annual Ascension Day procession of barges which 'surveyed the boundaries of the Tyne'. This led, by Victoria's time, to regular regattas on the stretch of the river above King's Meadow opposite Elswick. The individual sculling matches on the Tyne drew enormous crowds and the Newcastle Journal related that the river on such occasions was crowded with vessels of every description, but most conspicuously the Corporation and Trinity House barges 'crowded with fashionable company'. Such contests produced popular heroes, none more so than James Renforth from Newcastle who, like all genuine heroes, died young whilst actually boat racing. Renforth's funeral attracted 100,000 mourners thus closing the whole city for the day.

Other rowing craft had their speed trials, particularly the inshore fishing boats which vied for the best fisheries and most lucrative markets and, as with the Thames watermen, there were organized matches. A well-remembered race was between a Northumberland crew from Blyth and a Yorkshire crew from Staithes, both rowing the style of boat used by Grace Darling 30 years before — an old-fashioned coble. The race took place on 11 September 1866 and was promoted as the 'Great Coble Race from Staithes to Whitby' for a prize of £100 and a huge silver cup denoting the Championship of the North Sea. Crowds thronged to see the race over ten miles of open sea, but must have been disappointed at the result which was an easy win for the Yorkshiremen in one hour twenty-five minutes; so elated were the winners that they lifted up their heavy oars and danced on the seats. Such contests as this led eventually to the establishment of sea rowing clubs up and down the east coast and the inauguration of annual regattas which still take place.

West Country pilots were responsible for yet another form of rowing contest, competing with each other just as they did for business by rowing as much as 20 miles out to sea to secure a commission. The pilot gigs (*fig. 28*) were built for speed being 30 feet long, only four feet six inches in the beam and rowed by six oarsmen. Inevitably races between them evolved into established regattas, and with Ralph Bird at Devoran now building new racing gigs in the traditional style this antiquated sport has been secured for the future. Such rowing was not exclusive to men for there were many West Country fisherwomen and ferry-women, like Ann Glanville from Saltash, who were capable of taking on and beating men. Spurred on, perhaps, by the Queen's accession Ann Glanville formed a crew of women who competed at many small regattas on the River Tamar. They were so successful that they challenged male crews throughout the country, most notably in the north of England and Portsmouth. After success at Fleetwood Royal Regatta in 1849 they were presented to Queen Victoria and eventually competed in the Le Havre Regatta of 1850, not only winning but having rowed across the channel to take part!

Such trade-based contests were by no means restricted to rowing for wherever boats were used for work there would be races, contests, matches or regattas of some sort as entertainment and recreation. More importantly, however, they were sources of extra income for the contestants, who could win substantial prizes. Watermen punted for prize money in the eighteenth century and fishermen sailed for it from much earlier times, very often under royal patronage and occasionally with royalty on board and lending a hand. By Victoria's time fishermen's regattas had become commonplace around Britain's coasts, and were often the excuse for a general town holiday. The racing remained serious as at Worthing Fishermen's Regatta (*fig. 45*) where the courses were meticulously checked, tonnage precisely recorded and sailing methods umpired scrupulously from the committee's steamer. Here smacks from over 20 tons to under 6 tons could find a relevant class of race.

Social divisions and the amateur ethic

The tradition of working boats and trademen's regattas, often under the patronage of the gentry, gradually led to the use of similar boats by gentlemen amateurs and the establishment of the amateur ethic. Yachting was pioneered in Holland in the seventeenth century and introduced to England as a recreation by Charles II, who had spent nearly ten years in exile in the Netherlands. Together with his brother, the Duke of York, he made the racing of yachts fashionable. English nobility followed the fashion, often hiring professionals in the form of fishermen to helm for them in races for large stakes. By 1820 the Royal Yacht Club was well established as was the expensive and exclusive nature of the sport. In 1857 the America's Cup was inaugurated and the most famous British challenges were mounted by the Prince of Wales' friend, Sir Thomas Lipton, whose series of yachts named *Shamrock* bid for the cup five times between 1899 and 1930. Pleasure sailing remained the preserve of the rich until well after the Edwardian period but rowing for pleasure and recreation was already well established by 1837. Many public schools and Oxbridge colleges provided facilities for boating, and there were many boat hiring firms throughout the country that catered for increasing public enthusiasm (*fig. 50*). Town guides of the period, like that of Shrewsbury, would often mention aquatic excursions as attractions and encourage the hiring of boats at 'moderate charges' so that the delights of the riverside could be seen and enjoyed 'especially on a summer's evening when all is calm and serene'; in this particular instance a trip to the delightfully rural village of Uffington was recommended.

The popularity of boating for all classes was not restricted to the south of England nor to pleasant rural venues; in the North the centre for hiring was the Manchester or Salford area where as early as 1839 boats were available for hire at Mary Ann's on Victoria Bridge. Nearer the centre of town were the boathouses of George Pierce and Mark Addy, both professional scullers who encouraged the sport of rowing amongst amateurs and who established the Manchester and Salford Regatta Club. In Preston the local hirer was William Crooks, who established himself in Avenham Park in the 1850s; his success was primarily responsible for the setting up of no less than three amateur rowing clubs in the city (*fig. 60*). Similar tales can be told of many places in the country, some unlikely such as Wigan, Talkin Tarn, Birkenhead and Liverpool, and some more appropriate such as Nottingham, Huntingdon, Gloucester and Lincoln, but wherever the recreational side of rowing was carried on a competitive club would follow. These clubs suffered from the beginning in their constitutions which allowed all classes of men to compete together in the loosely organized regattas of the early Victorian period. As society fragmented during the mid-nineteenth century with the rising middle classes asserting themselves ever more vigorously the clubs and regattas introduced an amateur code which effectively barred manual workers from competing with 'gentlemen' (*fig. 36*). This cultural trend led eventually to the formation of the Amateur Rowing Association in 1883. The 'Amateur Question' had become the subject for leading articles in the *Times* which left no one in doubt of their position: 'The outsiders, artisans, mechanics and such like troublesome persons can have no place found for them. To keep them out is a thing desirable on every account. Let no base mechanic arms be suffered to thrust themselves in here!'

Fortunately for the 'base mechanics' a place was found for them by Frederick James Furnivall who founded the National Amateur Rowing Association in 1890 (*fig. 100*). Furnivall was an eccentric philologist whose academic work led ultimately to the definitive English dictionary and whose social conscience drove him to establish the London Working Men's College; he also founded the Hammersmith Sculling Club for Women. The NARA provided an infrastructure for the disenfranchised oarsman and its clubs and regattas (*fig. 85*) ran parallel with those of the ARA until their eventual coalition in 1956. By 1890 the number of rowing and boating clubs had risen to a staggering 301 in the London area and 457 nationwide. This was the high point of institutional boating as from this time onwards circumstances conspired to reduce the number of clubs. This was mainly because of the increasing seriousness of the competition brought about by the ARA, Henley Royal Regatta and the advent of international racing, together with new and scientific methods of training. Those who wished to continue racing under these conditions tended to join the bigger clubs and left the rest to become what we regard today as the archetypal Edwardian 'man in a boat'.

Pleasure boating, expeditions and etiquette

The split between boating for pleasure and boating as a sport owes a lot to fashion and that in turn relied almost entirely upon Henley Royal Regatta, which was inaugurated in 1839 as a commercial attraction for the sleepy old village of Henley on Thames. Following the first Varsity boat race there in 1829 it was felt that with proper management a regular event could be staged to everyone's advantage and very soon the larger London clubs were attending. Shortly after that the Prince of Wales took to coming during Ascot week bringing in his wake all the fashionably inclined of the day. To see and be seen it was necessary for all these people to take to boats of one sort or another during Henley week (*fig. 39*). It wasn't long, therefore, before a boating tradition was built up amongst a set of people who had time to spare and lived conveniently close to the Thames. Exploratory trips up the river became fashionable for a week-end break or even a short holiday. These trips were made as simple and carefree as possible with hotels springing up at strategic points along the route and carriage facilities for the return of the boat. As the railway network spread ever further, the Great Western Railway advertised combined rail and river excursions from Paddington. For only 1 guinea this excursion took passengers to Henley where they would embark on a steam launch on which they would spend the day cruising and enjoying lunch before returning to the Red Lion at Henley, dinner and rail home.

However such pampering did not suit all tastes and the appetites of the more adventurous were constantly whetted throughout the Victorian age with a succession of books and pamphlets relating some exciting excursion or other. Within the space of 50 years some 72 books had been published concerning some aspect of adventurous boating including, of course, the best-known one of all, *Three Men in a Boat,* published in 1889. Others ranged further than the homely old Thames, telling of trips through the Caledonian canal, the Solent, the Mersey and Severn rivers, yacht voyages around England, and even trips undertaken in Europe and the Near East, the best-known of which were those of John MacGregor. Like Furnivall, MacGregor was something of an eccentric with a social conscience and after Cambridge University where he rowed in the varsity boat set himself the task of clothing the poor and feeding the hungry of London. He raised money for his schemes by touring foreign waters in his home-made 'Rob Roy' canoe which was clinker built of cedar (to which was later added a mast and sail), and then writing and lecturing on his adventures. His *Tour of Europe* in 1865 and *Tour of Scandinavia* in 1866 were popular best sellers and his final book and lectures on his tour of the Middle East earned him £10,000 which he duly spent on his schools. MacGregor founded the Canoe Club in 1866 and for the next 30 years paddling and sailing canoes (*fig. 54*) was an extremely popular pastime. Yet by the early 1900s the paddling element had almost died out despite the number of clubs throughout the country. The sport of paddling was revived with the introduction from Germany of a new design of kayak which was more responsive to the paddle than the old-fashioned touring version; from this point canoeing went from strength to strength.

Given the Victorian obsession with outward appearance and attention to detail it is not surprising that the boating boom produced, in addition to the 72 volumes of adventure stories already mentioned, a further 31 volumes of a technical nature, many of which included sections on aquatic etiquette. The following excerpts will give us an idea of the age as exemplified by an editorial comment in *Lock to Lock Times* magazine which noted smugly that boating was truly the most aristocratic of sports and socially acceptable because it had not become 'the child of the bookmaker nor the pastime of the rowdy'. The same writer adds to this in a book written in 1898 by stating that the taking of exercise afloat is also the most scientific of sports. He carries on to develop an aquatic code of behaviour which contains such gems as Rule 6: 'It is shocking bad form to stand up in a boat' and Rule 8: 'Chaff is an excellent thing in its place – its proper place on the Thames is between Kingston waterworks and Moulsey Lock'. Some other writers had rather more practical advice to offer the eager oarsman especially with regard to women as in this comment from *The Boating Man's Vade Mecum* published in 1891: 'Consider the comfort of the lady in preference to exhibiting your skill as an oarsman and bear in mind that most serious and fatal accidents have arisen through women becoming frightened and jumping up at perilous moments.'

Punting developments

The number of books written on rowing and canoeing completely dwarfs those on punting, as between 1837 and 1910 there were only four published. This is not entirely surprising as punts were only known as working boats for most of the period. Even when they became used for other purposes punts were restricted to the Thames area, although by the Edwardian era they had spread to most of the major rivers of the kingdom. Traditionally punts had been used for river fishing and ballast punts for river dredging (*fig. 9*) whilst the larger variety were built for transporting cargoes or passengers in the numerous ferries throughout the country. The pleasure punts and racing punts of today were unknown before 1860. The Thames fishermen who used the most manageable of the traditional punts were often hired by the new breed of boating men and it was a short step from that to amateurs taking up the new form of boating, as the punt afforded a more stable and capacious platform for their social activities. Punt racing was instituted by the punt fishermen of the Thames who inaugurated the first championships in 1877 using ordinary fishing punts and for which, according to the *Maidenhead Advertiser,* 'a dense crowd had collected, the Londoners backing the Moulsey man for all they could get on'. The original stake was £40 but later Abel Beesley from Oxford (*fig. 79*) challenged the winner for considerably more and won by 'sixty or seventy yards'. Beesley went on to retain the championship every year until 1890, mainly because of his skill at 'pricking', a style of punting which involved remaining stationary and letting the pole slide through the hands rather than walking the length of the boat. Amateurs who had begun to enjoy punting as a social pastime took it up as a sport, with the foundation of the Thames Punting Club in 1885 which drew up rules and established the amateur championships in the same year.

Eccentricities

A curious footnote to the tale of punting is afforded by Lord Wolseley's expedition to the Nile region to relieve General Gordon at Khartoum. The peculiar nature of the Nile stream and its cataracts required the use of punt-style craft for the 370 mile journey to the head of Dongola province. Wolseley offered a prize of £100 to the first battalion to complete the course. (The *Times* called it the 'longest boat race in history'.) The punts were paddled rather than poled and this combination of styles was called dongola racing and was taken up as a fashionable event at Thames regattas (*fig. 97*). The first dongola race was held at Maidenhead in 1886 with crews of eight, four a side with canoe paddles.

Another method of navigating the Thames was with the gondola (*fig. 94*), built somewhat after the style of those in Venice with the 'crew' standing in the rear and backwatering his oar for propulsion. The main advantage was that it was far easier to see exactly where the craft was going and therefore much safer for the uninitiated boating man than the rowing skiff.

An Anglican clergyman, Edward Berthon, gave us the Berthon Collapsible Boat. Another rather eccentric mode of river travel was the water cycle (*fig. 98*) which made its appearance at the beginning of the Edwardian period and was widely advertised but never actually caught on in the popular imagination. The advantages lay in the 'cyclists' facing forward and its stability. The inventors planned on hosts of road cyclists taking to the water en masse—something which never happened and for which real boating men can be eternally grateful. Examples were seen and commented upon as here in a contemporary journal: 'From the water cycle which we saw lately on our metropolitan river a fair turn of speed was obtained. It was easily steered and made its way through the intricate paths of holiday traffic below Hampton Court in such a way as to outpace boats of an ordinary kind.'

The age of steam

With the development of steam power and the internal combustion engine the Edwardians became more and more interested in speed and applied this interest to boating. Both Victorians and Edwardians had always been fascinated with racing and competition because of their adventurous and acquisitive instincts and the steam boat did not evade their attention. The paddle steamer (*fig. 16*) could be regarded almost as a symbol of the Victorian age, bustling around the nation's coasts and rivers, working hard in all manner of ways and exuding an air of stability and power. As the steam engine became more refined it was fitted to smaller and smaller craft which became, in turn, a symbol of the cultured and leisured Edwardian age. The working boat had made the evolutionary transition to the pleasure craft and as technology improved this evolutionary trend was maintained with the application of the steam turbine to power boat racing. Private steam yachts were common by the 1870s and by 1888 Sir Alfred Harmsworth had presented the Harmsworth Cup for the power boat championships, won in that year with an average speed of 19.5 mph, relatively slow compared with subsequent steam turbine powered craft. The first of this craft, *Turbinia*, was timed at nearly 40 mph in 1897. Many time trials took place on Lake Windermere in Cumbria with many design improvements being tested and by 1907 we can see the modern style of power boat emerging in *Satanella* (*fig. 91*).

End of an era

The Edwardian era was not at all the period of aristocratic elegance of popular mythology but one of political tension and social division, a division which was as apparent on the boating scene as elsewhere in society. The plea made by the secretary of Bolton Rowing Club when asking 'is not a working man who is honest in all his dealings as much a gentleman as a man with a good coat on?' was countered categorically by the boating establishment. They replied that 'the facts that men of a lower class are well conducted and civil and have never competed for money are NOT sufficient to make a man a gentleman as well as an amateur'. The social apartheid evident in this retort was rigorously applied throughout the boating scene in all its forms and caused much ill-feeling both then and since with Henley Royal Regatta; the Regatta refused to drop its ban against manual workers until 1938, and then only grudgingly. Royal patronage of yachting and canoeing and regular attendance at Henley only served to widen the gap between the gentleman and the hired man who punted, rowed or helmed for him – even Henley Royal Regatta itself was dependent on scores of time-served watermen who were paid by the day to police the course (*fig. 7*) and enclosures and stand in full regalia to open doors for members in the Leander Club. Their boating had been unrelenting hard work whilst that of the leisured classes was, in Kenneth Grahame's immortal phrase, 'simply messing about'; the whole world which lay between this diligence and dilettantism was brought abruptly to an end by the First World War and the boating boom died with the millions.

GLOSSARY

Canadian canoe   A totally open canoe used for fishing and touring derived from the style used by Canadian Indians and paddled with a single-bladed paddle.

Coracle   Perhaps the oldest craft still in daily operation: resembling an open umbrella with a cross seat almost amidships and constructed of woven willow laths covered with animal skins and later tarred canvas. The boatman uses a single paddle about five feet long.

Dongola   Merely a pleasure punt paddled rather than punted by a crew of two, four or six often half men, half women.

Eton skiff   A lighter, narrower skiff intended for racing (also known as 'Funnies').

Fine sculls or 'best boats'   These were longer and narrower than whiffs with sliding seats and longer outriggers designed specifically for competition. Refinements are still continuing.

Gig   An open rowing boat at one time popular on inland waterways especially on the Thames although declining in popularity after the 1860s. It was made of clinker (overlapping plank) construction with a straight side below the gunwales. It had a fixed seat and was inrigged.

Gondola   The well-known Venetian craft used in Venice for passenger and cargo work. Adapted for the shallow waters of the lagoon its usual length is between 30 and 40 feet. It is flat-bottomed with high curving stern and bows. The crew propels it from the stern by means of a single 'push' oar. It was popular in Edwardian England for its novelty value.

Kayak   A further development towards speed and manoeuvrability. This vessel derived from the boat used by the Eskimos for fishing and was completely decked out to exclude water with only a torso size cockpit to allow for crew. Shorter than the other varieties it was also narrower and inherently unstable; using a double paddle it is used specifically for racing.

Luggers, ketches and yawls   These are all sailing boats identified only by their rigging variations which are too esoteric to mention.

Pairs, fours and eights   These were racing boats for two, four and eight people still built on overlapping plank principles for the most part but with sliding seats and outriggers for speed. They were very long and narrow.

Pleasure punt   About the middle of the nineteenth century punts became popular for pleasure purposes and the working punt was modified by being made lighter with more overhang at the ends thus making them easier to propel. In addition, these punts would be fitted with mast and sail if required.

Pontoon   Derived from the early dug out canoe, the pontoon was flat-bottomed and square ended; it was used as a ferry and to support a floating bridge.

Racing punt   The ultimate modification for speed in competition: the over-hang at the ends became extreme and the width narrowed to the length of a man's foot. Some 30 feet long and only 6 or 7 inches deep they can be pro-pelled at almost incredible speeds.

Rob Roy canoe   Designed by 'Rob Roy' MacGregor, an adaptation of the Canadian Canoe for use in expedition work. He installed a weatherproof decking over three quarters of the vessel and made provision for a mast and sail. It was paddled with a double bladed paddle.

Severn trow   A modification of the original barge pulled by horses or (more often) men. The bows were cut away to deflect the severe Severn tide and the depth increased for the same reason, together with a desire for more cargo room and increased stability. The original square sail was replaced with a schooner rig for greater adaptability to the changing winds.

Skiff   A popular pleasure boat which replaced the gig being lighter, shorter and narrower but similar in other respects. Whilst the gig was primarily a working boat the skiff was for pleasure only.

Thames sailing barge   Similar in derivation to the trow but modified for Thames conditions. A wider, shallower boat it was used for work in the many tidal creeks feeding the main river. Like the trow the Thames barge can be manhandled by a crew of two using huge sweep oars and punting poles and can be used as a 'lighter' taking cargoes from other deeper draught boats (and thus lightening them).

Wherry   Primarily seen on the Thames and derived from the old boats used as ferries by eighteenth century watermen. It had practically died out by the First World War. They were long and wide with high pointed bows often sheathed in iron (sometimes known as 'iron noses'). Some were pointed at the stern and could be rowed in either direction. These boats were the first boats to be raced by the watermen but as the racing got more professional they were refined into whiffs.

Whiff   This was a narrow sculling boat, about 23 feet long and only 16 inches or so wide, still clinker built, originally inrigged but by the 1840s out-rigged for greater speed. These were superseded by fine sculls.

Working punt or 'rough' punt   This derived from the pontoon but was smaller and narrower and consequently more manoeuvrable. It was used for all types of river work including fishing, weeding and de-silting.

1 One of the old and redundant Severn sailing barges or trows pictured permanently moored in the countryside a few miles south of Bewdley in Worcestershire. Although not attributed, the scene is almost certainly the owner's family – his wife and five daughters – and the family servants enjoying a summer afternoon picnic. These barges were so well-built that even today they can be seen often converted to house boats. At the time of this photograph in 1876, however, many barges were derelict and useless, their cargoes taken by rail.

2 The last Severn sailing barge pictured just below Ironbridge in Shropshire during the late 1870s. In the
eighteenth and early nineteenth centuries these barges
would have dominated this scene whilst waiting to
unload at the wharves above the bridge. They were raced
by their masters into and out of Bristol port and were
occasionally entered for the sailing regattas in the
estuary. But by the middle of the nineteenth century they
had been totally superseded by the railway.

3 The steamship *Powerful* called into service to pull a horse and carriage across on the Windermere ferry *Mary Anne* in 1879. Before the introduction of the steam chain ferry in 1870 generations of row ferries were used to form the link between Hawkshead and Bowness (for Kendal). The ferry pictured here was used as a back-up service until the 1940s, sometimes being drawn by a steam launch. The boat was propelled by huge sweep oars supported on gigantic outriggers and rowed by only one man.

4 The boathouse at Bonnyrigg Hall in Northumberland *c*.1880. Every country house of a substantial size during this period would have or aspire to have a lake or river frontage; often a lake would be dug specially or a hollow flooded so that fish could be stocked and house guests enjoy a pleasant afternoon fishing and boating. More often a substantial boathouse would be built: in the South this took the form of a two storey pavilion with lounge above and dock below; in the North it was more usually a no-nonsense boat store used primarily for the game keeper's working boats.

5 The Sunderland Point ferryman pictured in 1880.
Sunderland Point lies at the very mouth of the River
Lune and is cut off by the tide twice a day. The ferryman
assumed, therefore, a greater than normal importance,
but even so he would probably have divided his time between ferrying, fishing and boat repair work. For work
close into the shore, as here, most boatmen would
employ the single blade sculling action.

6 A Company or State barge laid up on the River Isis in
Oxford probably before being used during Eights Week.
The precise date is unknown but likely to be in the 1880s
because that was the decade during which College rowing became most popular. This particular barge has a
larger state-room than usual and consequently fewer
rowing positions – only 12. Earlier versions, built for
genuine transport, would have a small cabin and up to
40 oarsmen.

7 The procession of Watermen pulled by a Thames Conservancy steamer at Henley Royal Regatta, July 1882, with Fawley Court in the background. These time-served watermen, wearing their badges of office, were hired by the regatta stewards for the whole week to police the event and keep the course free from the thousands of water-borne spectators.

8 Two Morecambe fishermen laying whammeling nets to catch the early tide and the larger shoals. A whammel net is a long corked net strung out from the bow of the boat bellied out by the ebb tide and pulled back aboard. Two men are needed for the operation – one to pull on the extra length fishing blades, one to fish – and the whammel boats are designed for fore and aft stability during the operation. This boat is of local design and they are still being built in Morecambe. The photo was taken in the 1880s off the River Lune estuary near Sunderland Point.

9 Dredging operations on the River Thames at
Abingdon in the 1880s. Although steam-powered dredging was possible it was far cheaper at this time to continue using man power for a stretch of water now little
used commercially except for the dwindling Oxford-
Reading trade. It is more likely that the men were de-silting for the increasing numbers of pleasure craft because
a contemporary account tells us that 'the stream here is
apprenticed to pleasure, the pleasure of a rapid and rest-
less escape from work in offices and shops'.

10 Some canal boats ready to pass through the Hanwell
Locks from the Grand Junction Canal to the River Brent
and from there to the Thames at Brentford where cargoes would be transhipped to the larger river 'punts' and
barges of the London river system. These locks were
always busy because they represented one of the links
between the national canal system and the River
Thames, but Hanwell is interesting also as a meeting
point of canal, river, road and rail. Even here in the
1880s it is apparent that rail has made an impact as in
the canal heyday this scene would have been dominated
by huge numbers of craft queuing to pass through the
locks.

11 At a time when the protection of trade routes around the world was a national pre-occupation the first series of modern battleships made its appearance: this is the ill fated *Victoria* being towed from the shipyard at Elswick on the River Tyne in 1887. Still only partially armour-plated she was later rammed by the *Camperdown* during what was officially described as 'an injudicious man-oeuvre' in the eastern Mediterranean, and sank with the loss of 370 crew. The men who built her in the Elswick yards were the stalwarts of the many rowing clubs on the Newcastle stretch of the Tyne and these waters often featured as the venue for the world championships in scul-ling and rowing.

12 Bridlington harbour in Yorkshire pictured in 1889. An interesting scene for its variety of craft: a
working two-masted schooner, used
for deep sea fishing, a selection of
single masters for coastal fishing
and recreation, a rowing boat for a
trip around the harbour (from a letting yard behind the harbour wall)
and two paddle steamers taking
holiday makers on the time-hon-
oured 'trip around the bay'. The
steamers worked in the River
Humber as tug boats and came to
Bridlington for extra income when
business was slack.

13 A dramatic view of the North Shields fishing fleet taken in 1891. These lug-rigged craft could be sailed by two men and when working would often travel many miles in search of the herring shoals. Their huge ochre sails could also be seen in local fishermen's regattas up and down the north-east coast when the best sailors challenged each other for cash prizes. These regattas would occasionally include races in the small boats or 'kogges' for wives who were generally skilled in the art of single stern oar sculling. In mid-channel can be seen a paddle steamer acting as tug to a deep sea schooner; such steamers would often double up as pleasure craft at Whitley Bay and Cullercoats when business was slack. When this photograph was taken every other man in Shields was a fisherman or sailor – today no one is.

14 A view of the River Nidd and high level bridge at
Knaresborough, North Yorkshire. Since the eighteenth
century this spot has been popular for boating, and this
picture, taken in 1892, shows some working boats as well
as the usual selection of punts, canoes and rowing boats
available for hire. The tub punts were regularly used for
all manner of river work and occasionally for net fishing
where this was allowed and poaching where it was not.
Here the men are clearing the river of the heavy summer
weed.

15 H.M. yacht *Enchantress* sailing from Trafford wharf for Mode Wheel and the opening by Queen Victoria of the Manchester Ship Canal on 21 July 1894. The building of the canal and the development of Salford Docks effectively killed a variety of amateur and professional boating clubs which have never been revived. Boating as a pastime was continued on Trafford Park Lake until that too was brought to an end by the establishment of the new industrial estate after the First World War. There were, however, regular bank holiday steamer trips down the canal, and although these too died out between the wars they have recently been revived.

16 The Liverpool ferry on the way to Birkenhead in 1895. This ferry, the *Rock Ferry* was one of the most heavily used and regularly updated because of the development of the Birkenhead docks and shipyards which can be seen in the background. For anyone familiar with this stretch of water it is almost impossible to believe that the old Rock Ferries were propelled by arm power alone. Mersey Rowing Club, whose headquarters used to be on this stretch of water, moved out to avoid the increasing river traffic – the ferry alone ran through the day at 15 minute intervals! On the left can be seen the paddle steamer which was used for the New Brighton run.

17 This view of Westminster in 1895 shows the River
Thames equivalent of the Severn trow. The loaded boats
are punts which varied in capacity – the maximum was
50 tons – and were the workhorses of the Edwardian
Thames. The larger barges ranged up to 120 tons and
were propelled by tide and wind (note the hinged mast
on the far boat for negotiating bridges. They were
manned by lightermen capable of rowing with 30 foot
oars. This art of navigation was known as 'driving under
oars' and was unique to Britain. It required enormous
skill in manoeuvring huge loads under bridges at all
states of the tide.

18 Boating at the interface: Kingston upon Thames in
1896 showing a mixture of working and pleasure craft
mingling at the main venue for up and down river traffic.
The coal barges were unable to use the upper river as
they were too large to negotiate the locks or shallows;
they were able, however, to pass through Teddington
lock which was the largest on the river system. (Note that
the derivation of Teddington is from 'tide's end town'.)
The steam pleasure launches restricted themselves to the
Royal River upstream and avoided the difficulties of
navigation on the downstream London river.

19 & 20 Two ketch rigged working boats: *Attempt* making good way into Cowes in 1898 and a fishing smack pictured in 1910 with every ounce of sail aloft racing to be first into Ramsgate harbour and the fish auctions. *Attempt* was well known locally for her speed and carried general cargoes anywhere along the south coast; the rig was managed with a fair degree of ease by a master and a boy, who can just be seen in this photograph atop the mizzen mast. Both boats are pulling along the usual working boat which was propelled by a single stern scull.

21 'Speed bonny boat like a bird on the wing . . . over the sea to Skye'. The ferryman waits for his passengers (and the photographer) before setting out for Harlosh on 20 October 1900. The group comprises Mr and Mrs Heathcote and their children, Mrs Macleod and her daughter; Mr Macleod is the photographer. A birthday trip like this was an adventure in those days – mechanical ferries did not arrive in this part of the world until well after the First World War.

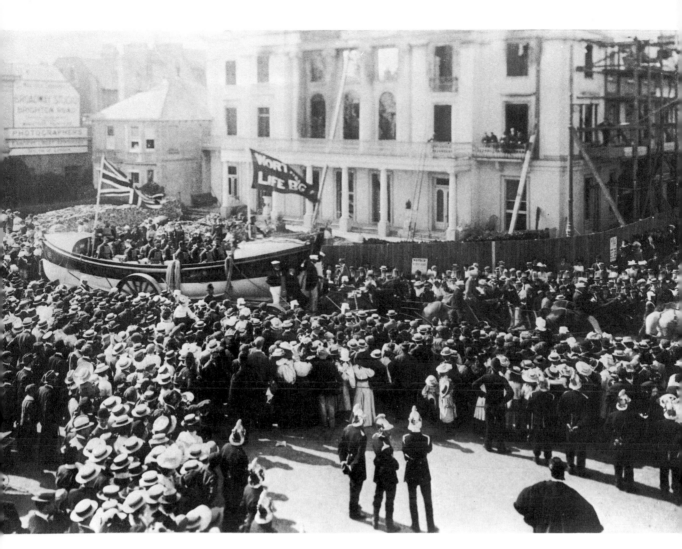

22 The Worthing lifeboat *Richard Coleman* and crew in a
procession celebrating the new boat given by Mrs Birt-
Davies Coleman on 7 August 1901. At this time there
were only pulling lifeboats available to the RNLI which
were occasionally sail assisted. Despite many technical
developments similar boats (as at Whitby) were still in
regular use in the 1950s.

23 (*left*) The ferryman and his family at Uffington, five miles down river from Shrewsbury, on the River Severn pictured in 1902 probably returning from Sunday morning church. Such rope ferries were common on fast flowing rivers such as the Severn and the ferrymen often supplemented their meagre incomes by turning out at local regattas to row, scull or punt for the cash prizes on offer.

24 (*above*) A picture of the last Runcorn ferryman taken in 1905. There had been a ferry at this point on the River Weaver since Norman times. By the early Victorian period traffic was particularly brisk with passengers using it as access to the new St Helen's and Runcorn Gap railway. In 1865 the ferry was bought by the London and Northwest Railway Company and the tolls increased to 2d. (two old pence) a trip, but in 1868 the company built a bridge which incorporated a footpath and the ferry business naturally declined. The construction of the Transporter road bridge in 1905 finished it hence this valedictory photograph of Mr Harrison.

25 The old and the new berthed together at Runcorn on
the Manchester Ship Canal in 1905, the year that the
Transporter bridge in the background was built. Such
tugs as these were used by the Canal Company extensively to help the larger ships through the locks and to
berth them, but they were also used to haul the old sailing barges the whole way if the wind decided not to blow.
This state of affairs could not and did not last: some of
the sturdier barges had engines fitted and the rest were
discarded.

26 Narrow boats unloading bricks at Cheddleton on the Caldon canal near Leek in Staffordshire, 1906. These craft superseded the old sailing barges as the canals themselves replaced the many treacherous rivers. The sailing skills and watermanship required by the boat-masters were irrelevant to the new canalmen, who could travel great distances fully loaded and guarantee delivery to the hour. As they in turn were made redundant by the railways the canals became the scene of a new generation of pleasure boating enthusiasts.

27 The steam ship *Linnet* on the Crinan canal in 1907; the major use for such steam vessels at this time was passenger carrying either in the capacity of a ferry or as a pleasure cruiser for the increasing numbers of tourists. The tourists flocked to areas boasting some royal associations and so Scotland and the Isle of Wight were favourite targets during this period.

28 The pilot gig *Slippen* at Newquay before setting out to collect bodies from the wreck of the *Thomas W. Lawson* in 1907. The stern sail was a common addition to these craft and improved their already considerable speed. Jack Hicks, the last of the gig pilots, is standing third from the stern.

29 A 12 oared Admiralty cutter pictured near Calstock on the River Tamar in 1910. Such boats were used as small boat transport for ship's captains or as official transport for coastguards who occasionally needed the eight to ten knots that such boats could attain with a fit crew. Only such boats were allowed 12 oars as other craft were restricted to six following the eighteenth century bye-law which allocated the slower boats to all potential smugglers. This boat was probably made by Jim Goss and Sons who had a yard at Calstock.

30 The enormous popularity of the Isle of Wight as a holiday area promoted by royal patronage and the Royal Yacht Club necessitated modernization of the various ferries which serviced the community. This shot of the steam chain ferry between East and West Cowes in 1910 is typical of those taking over from the old boatmen of the nineteenth century. The reduction of the manual skills of watermanship associated with, for example, ferrying, pilotage, lighterage, river maintenance and fishing because of the advance of steam and petrol meant that the professional side of competitive boating, whether rowing, sailing or punting went into terminal decline before the First World War.

31 Mr Bryams and family of Belfield, Bowness on
Windermere enjoying a leisurely afternoon on board
Linnet in 1870. Her engine was made by Plenty and Son
of Newbury and she was typical of many steam launches
used by their lakeside owners for picnicking in quiet bays
and steaming peacefully about Lake Windermere before
the days of the environmental lobby.

32 Ladies sculling on the River Severn at Shrewsbury in 1880. Perhaps they had read *The Gentlewomen's Book of Sports* published that year by Lady Greville in which she says that 'It is essential for every English girl to learn to row; twenty years ago it was not considered "comme il faut" for a lady to row but now everything is changed and it is clearly to be seen that it is the very best thing for her.'

33 Four young ladies in a double skiff at
Hartford having sculled two miles down the
River Ouse from Huntingdon. They probably rented the boat from Childs by the
town bridge and will undoubtedly take tea
in the village before turning homewards.
The scene is taken during the 1880s and
apart from its charm the photograph shows
the enthusiasm with which women took to
boating as one expression of their increasing
independence during this decade. Most
boating clubs admitted women as full members before the turn of the century.

34 & 35 Two views of Bewdley in Worcestershire taken
in 1881: the large pontoon on the left by the bridge (supported by two old trows) was the headquarters of the
Bewdley Rowing Club. It was towed to Stourport in
October and returned in March each year ready for the
boating season. Up river from the bridge is the old town
quay where the barges used to load cargoes of pot clay,
glass, iron ware and hides; the grooves of the haulage
ropes can still be seen on the bridge supports. By 1881 it
is apparent that there is no industrial trade at all and
that the river has been taken over by pleasure boating.
The George Hotel advertised itself as a centre for boating
and fishing holidays renting out its fleet of rowing boats
and organizing steam boat excursions up and down the
river.

36 Liverpool Victoria Rowing Club members pictured in 1884, their inaugural year. It was made up of local tradesmen who could not gain entry to the Mersey Rowing Club because of the Rowing Association's strict definition of 'amateur'. The club soon became a force to be reckoned with in regional and national competition and recently it provided the sport with its first provincial president.

37 A Cambridge river party made up of members of the
City of Cambridge Rowing Club pictured in Bait's Bite
Lock on the River Cam en route for tea at Clayhithe in
1886. The barge *James Fisher* was named after the founder
of the famous Cambridge boat hiring firm who had been
instrumental in establishing the club in 1844.

38 A view of the River Isis in Oxford during the summer Eights Week of 1887. The Eights Week traditionally swept away the examination blues and provided an atmosphere of relaxation for thousands of spectators invited aboard the College barges. The picture shows the proliferation of craft common in this era: the Canadian canoe, single and double skiffs and a variety of punts as well as the eights themselves.

39 (*above*) Teatime at Henley Regatta, July 1887. Although this is a well-known scene it does indicate very effectively how popular boating had become. Royal patronage had made the event itself uncomfortably fashionable and so the stewards were discussing how to deter competitors and spectators alike from attending! Single, double and treble skiffs, Rob Roy canoes, Canadian canoes, punts, house boats and a gondola can all be seen.

40 (*right*) A tranquil scene on the Preston to Kendal canal taken in 1888 on the Aldcliffe stretch coming into Lancaster from the south. The canal had long been unused by commercial traffic and the main line railway extensions of the 1870s had taken what little Port of Lancaster trade remained. Interestingly the main local promoter of the rail extensions was Edmund Sharpe, president of the local rowing club. The extension released the canal for pleasure boating, an example of which is pictured here. It is unusual for a Victorian photograph to show a lady rowing whilst a gentleman steers!

41 A novel seaside photograph of James Howarth and
his family on holiday in the Isle of Man in 1889, probably posed in the photographer's studio. Mr Howarth,
with the pipe, was a sign writer from Bury who was following the upper working class trend of taking a week's
holiday in July. He must have been more prosperous
than most as the Isle of Man was considered to be rather
expensive.

42 One man in a boat at Runnymeade in 1890 heading
for Windsor and all points west. This Thames double
skiff has been modified for camping and the hoops and
canvas can be seen in the stern; perhaps this lone sculler
was encouraged to take to the water by *Three Men in a
Boat*, published the year before. These Thames skiffs
were very durable craft and one of this era was sold
recently for £1,000 at an auction in Wiltshire.

43 The beach at Sandown on the Isle of Wight in 1890.
Sandown was the last island resort to be developed, but
the number of bathing machines shows how popular it
had become by this time. On the shore there are some inrigged pleasure boats together with some very modern
outrigged craft, two fishing smacks after a very old Dutch
design and, in the foreground, an old pilot gig. This gig
would have been used for fishing trips in the bay and its
owner is standing by looking at the camera; the horse
was used to beach the boat after each trip.

44 Tea aboard Colonel Ridehalgh's steam yacht *Britannia* after a Windermere Royal Yacht Club race in 1891. The yacht was a schooner rigged with two masts and fitted with 20 horse power engines which could propel her at 16 mph. The cabins were exquisitely panelled and the Colonel had commissioned special china and cutlery for catering on board. She was the scene of many celebrity parties in the years immediately before the First World War, but was broken up in 1916. She was probably the most opulent vessel ever to grace Lake Windermere.

45 (above) Worthing pier on Regatta Day, 15 August 1892: 'A regatta confined to watermen and fishermen of Worthing and members of the local rowing clubs was held today with a public subscription of £100. The sons of the sea have many good friends in the town with Sir Henry Fletcher M.P. present on the pier and Lady Fletcher graciously presenting the prizes. The sport was watched by a large concourse of people brought in by special trains run at low fares by the Rail Company. The pier was thronged by 3,700 persons passing through the turnstiles.' (*South Coast Mercury* newspaper.)

46 (*right*) The pleasure boating boom which lasted from the 1870s to the First World War was responsible for many municipal boating lakes throughout the country, particularly in the industrial towns where vast new parks were laid out for the recreation of the masses. Some councils saw the commercial value of such facilities and this picture shows the new marine lake at Southport, Lancashire in 1893. It was designed to beat the tide and encourage the boating fraternity to come to the resort more frequently and to stay longer. The Improvement and Foreshore Committee built a clubhouse for the local boating club on the lake and successfully encouraged new boating clubs to establish themselves in the town. Today there are still sailing and rowing clubs on the lake and regular summer regattas.

47 (*above*) Kaiser Wilhelm II disembarking from *Maru*, the Earl of Lonsdale's steam launch, at Waterside on Lake Windermere in 1895. Also in the picture are the three best-known passenger steamers of the time: *Dodo*, *Elfin* and *Tern* and two Windermere class yachts. Apparently the Kaiser was astonished at the speed of 20 knots which the *Maru* achieved on the way from Bowness.

48 (*right*) An interesting photograph of a working steam paddle boat – the Isle of Wight ferry steaming out of Lymington harbour – with an example of the new generation of steam pleasure craft in the foreground: a yacht just in name as the masts served decorative purposes only. The ferry is towing a cargo or haulage punt and the date is placed as 1896.

49 Worthing Regatta, 3 September 1898: 'Itinerant vendors were pitching their stalls on the shingle: a portly lady with her attractive wares, an outre gentleman scattering largesse in the shape of showing jewelry and others offering mysterious packages in a lottery; a clown on stilts, a conjuror, a mind reader and many other alfresco entertainments.' (*The Worthing Intelligence* newspaper.) Coastal regattas were so much more than mere competition!

50 With the growth of the railway network and the increasing fashion for boating, the River Thames in particular became a playground for all classes of people. Thames Ditton, pictured here in 1898, was well served by rail connections, close to expanding Surbiton and only a mile from Hampton Court Palace. Therefore the Swan did a roaring trade in renting out boats of all kinds. Along with many other such establishments they hired out camping boats – double skiffs modified to take iron or cane hoops over which canvas was stretched. These would be used for extended trips of seven or ten days up river, after which the excursionist would return by rail leaving the boats to be ferried home by watermen. Thames Conservancy figures for this year show that 10,482 pleasure boats were registered and 257,307 lock tickets were sold.

51 (*above*) A Nemesis Rowing Club sculler in regulation straw boater pictured on the River Irwell towards the centre of Salford in Lancashire at a point where the river enters Peel Park, in 1899. Rowing activity faded on this stretch of water because of increased industrial development and consequent river pollution. The University of Salford now occupies this area of the town and hosts a thriving boat club of its own, utilising the now much cleaner waters of the 'murky Irwell' and the commercially derelict Ship Canal.

52 (*right*) Captain Howard Blackburn, pictured with his yacht *Great Western* in Gloucester, docks after his single-handed passage from Gloucester, Massachusetts in 1899. The popularity of such trips was because of the publicity surrounding the first single-handed circumnavigation of the world by Joshua Slocum in 1895. What made Blackburn's trip so special was that he had lost his fingers through frost bite on a fishing trip. He designed his *Great Western* himself – a 30 foot sloop rigged yacht and he took 60 days to complete the trip.

53 (*above*) Boating on the River Irwell near Douglas Green Weir at Kersal near Salford in 1900. The scene shows the mansions of the local millowners in the still rural Kersal Vale and their flat-capped workers enjoying some Sunday afternoon recreation.

54 (*right*) The Rector of All Saints Church, St Ives in Cambridgeshire, in his Rob Roy canoe pictured in front of his church in 1900. This type of boat, with detachable fore sail, had been popular with the lone enthusiast ever since the well-publicised exploits of John MacGregor during the 1860s and 70s when he made several trips in Europe, Scandinavia and the Suez region. He designed his own boats and called them all *Rob Roy* after his famous ancestor. Single handed he was responsible for the rise of canoeing as a popular pastime and sport and founded the Royal Canoe Club in 1866.

55 (*above*) This scene in 1901 depicts a church outing from Thrapston at the Denford boathouse just a mile downstream on the River Nene in Northants. H. J. Groom was the ferryman at Denford who supplemented his income with boatbuilding, letting and general handiwork around the local villages. 'Messing about in boats' had received a boost with Jerome K. Jerome's *Three Men in a Boat* in 1889 and it was still possible for people like Groom to make a living. Sadly the First World War killed off many such businesses.

56 (*right*) Bracebridge landing stage on the River Witham, close to Lincoln, pictured in 1902. The building on the left was a public house and the wooden hut was the payment kiosk for the boats. It is typical of many such locations where public houses utilised their proximity to water to rent out boats and increase custom and turnover. The First World War was mainly responsible for killing off this public and recreational side of boating.

57 The floating cafeteria on the River Nidd at Knaresborough in North Yorkshire pictured in 1903. For centuries people have visited Knaresborough to see its
castle, visit the riverside and consult the local family of
fortune tellers. It was left to the Edwardians to see the
potential of a floating restaurant and bar; unfortunately
this floating facility failed to continue floating because of
lack of maintenance in the First World War and it was
never replaced.

58 *Boadicea*, seen here in 1905 reversing engines to berth at Lambeth Pier, was one of half-a-dozen paddle steamers run by the London and Westminster Steamboat Company and plying the stretches of river between Kew and Gravesend. For half-a-century the bulk of their business was with commuters, but the enormous development of the underground system had diminished this trade so much that by this time they were employed mostly in ferrying day trippers to the tourist sites.

59 Boulter's Lock near Maidenhead, a famous boating
rendezvous, pictured in 1905. The trip from Maidenhead
to Cookham Dene and back was a favourite Victorian
excursion and a busy Sunday afternoon at the lock
served as the lively subject for a marvellous painting by
E. J. Gregory, completed in 1895. This stretch of river
provided Kenneth Grahame with the material for *Wind in
the Willows* published in 1908: for example Quarry Wood
at Cookham Dene becomes the 'Wild Wood' and Clive-
don, 'Toad Hall'. This photograph and Gregory's painting epitomize pleasure boating in the Victorian and
Edwardian eras.

60 A summer Sunday afternoon in 1905 on the River
Ribble in Preston. Since the 1860s William Crooks and
his family had rented out boats from this spot in
Avenham Park and, as this picture of 75 people rowing
indicates, they were hugely successful. A combination of
several drownings, river silt and the First World War
closed the business, but the Boathouse Inn remains to
tell the tale.

61 Ishmael Lithgoe, the founder member of Agecroft Rowing Club, Salford, pictured here on his eightieth birthday in 1906 starting out on his daily outing. He had begun his rowing career with the Nemesis R.C. of Manchester but following the increase of river traffic in the city centre he founded the new club in the tranquil setting of Drinkwater Park, seven miles upstream, in 1861.

62 A well-posed scene of committee members at Talkin Tarn Rowing Club near Carlisle. This sole Cumbrian club is one of the few that row on lakes; it derived much of its income from letting out its pleasure boats to the general public. By 1907, when this picture was taken, it had 22 letting boats and club records show that 9,520 people used them during that year. No wonder that the *East Cumberland News* could say that 'To trace the influence of the club on the popularity of the town (Brampton) would be a work of supererogation.'

63 & 64 One of Nottingham Boat Club's summer water parties pictured in Holme Lock on the River Trent in August 1908. These parties were all male affairs and tended to terminate at some well-known hostelry. Once a season the ladies were treated to a picnic. The venue of Holme Lock has particular interest as it lies today adjacent to the mult-million pound Holme Pierrepont water sports centre which has hosted two World Rowing Championships. The on-shore picture shows the same party indulging in some dry land rowing, always a great favourite amongst boating men.

65 Kennet's Mouth in Reading where the Rivers Kennet
and Thames meet; headquarters of the local yacht club
and, on this occasion, the committee enclosure for the
Working Men's Regatta of 1909. The regatta had been
established in 1877 and was promoted by the Mayor and
Corporation; it received Royal patronage in 1896 which
accounts for the crest just discernible on the regatta
notice by the railings. The event was popular enough for
the town to be given a half-day holiday and for Huntley
and Palmer's biscuit factory to be closed for the day.

66 The Talkin Tarn Rowing Club senior four, with club trophies, making ready to join the Brampton Town Carnival in June 1910. The local rowing clubs particularly supported such events, especially in the more rural locations, in order to advertise their existence, encourage membership and raise funds. This is still quite common in the coastal resorts of southern England, the West Country, Whitby and Lancaster.

67 Trent Bridge, Nottingham, in 1910 indicating the popularity of boating in the city. The picture was taken from the Nottingham and Union boat house and shows the club's pleasure boats in the foreground together with their president's steam launch. Also prominent is the pleasure steamer which took the public to Colwick Park and back for one shilling, including the entrance fee. At this time there were four well-established boating clubs in the city.

68 Houseboats on the Thames at Henley in preparation
for the regatta of 1910. Some of these were on permanent
moorings but most were towed by steam launches on to
their annual sites, many from Oxford colleges and the
rest from the larger down river clubs. They would serve
as club barges where crews and supporters could receive
hospitality and enjoy the social aspects of the event
which had, for the majority, taken precedence over the
competition. During the Edwardian era there were over
80 such houseboats regularly gathered at the regatta and
private owners would bid for the prime spots along the
course and endeavour to ensure that the *Lock to Lock
Times* containing the vital social information was
promptly and currently delivered.

69 With the advent of the shorter working week and the Saturday half-holiday, workers like these from Trencherfield Mill, Wigan, could get out and about on canals which were free from the week day working traffic. The S. S. Thomas started life as a working steam barge bringing in bulk raw materials from Liverpool, and is seen here in 1910 ending its life on pleasure trips to Shevington, Parbold and Haigh Park. This area of Wigan Pier is now an award winning museum and tourist attraction.

70 Another example of how widespread 'messing about in boats' had become by 1910. Boating was one of the few occupations in which the whole family could indulge together and wherever water was available, however seemingly unsuitable, it was likely that some form of the activity would be encouraged for sport or profit. Such scenes as this would inevitably feature mixed groups in Sunday best dress as family expeditions would take place between morning and evening church; this group typifies the trend with Mr Henshall and his large family on the upper reaches of the River Mersey in Didsbury.

71 (*above*) Tom Bircy, one of Stratford-on-Avon Boat Club's first members, pictured in front of the field which now boasts the Memorial Theatre. Although taken in 1878 the photograph shows the development of the single sculling boat which had already evolved into the pencil thin craft shown here. As with most early club photographs Tom is wearing full rowing uniform: regulation shorts, rowing zephyr (athletic vest) and straw boater in club colours; failure to wear the uniform resulted in a fine.

72 (*right*) Berwick-on-Tweed Rowing Club and members pictured on 1 May 1881 – the first day of the boating season. Mr Spence, the full time boatman, sits on the foreshore; he was paid ten shillings a week as boatman and his wife two shillings for scrubbing the club room floor. A new-fangled sliding seat sculling boat is proudly and prominently displayed as a contrast to the old-fashioned heavy gigs tied up on shore.

73 (*left*) Sea cadets pulling up to the training ship H.M.S. *Ganges* after a series of ship's gig races – June 1885. The *Ganges* was permanently moored in the estuary of the River Fal in Cornwall and trained many generations of budding midshipmen.

74 (*above*) Ryde Rowing Club regatta of 1885 and the start of the mixed crew event from the Fishermen's Steps on Ryde Pier. The clubhouse and club flag are conspicuous with club secretary Henry Osborne on the lower steps watching his daughter Gertrude and son Jack taking part in the sixth boat from the camera.

75 Mersey Rowing Club Headquarters pictured in 1885 near the Birkenhead terminus of the Rock Ferry. The club was formed 40 years before by the gentleman of the Wirral, who stipulated that correct dress must always be worn – hence the oarsmen's caps and club blazers. Heavy river traffic forced the club into the docks themselves and finally to Chester. Although disbanded in the 1950s the club has been re-established recently in the new Liverpool docks complex.

76 Skiff racing at Gloucester Rowing Club in July 1885.
The rowing club had lately moved on to this stretch of
water on the Gloucester and Berkeley canal from the tur-
bulent waters of the Severn at Sandhurst. As the canals
were commercially superseded by rail they became
increasingly available for recreational boating. This
straight stretch of 1,000 yards at Gloucester was ideal for
rowing, skiffing, canoeing and punting.

77 The Oxford and Cambridge varsity boat race at
Barnes Bridge in 1886. Cambridge, the eventual winners
by two-thirds of a length, are ahead. It is almost impossible for us to imagine the huge interest shown by all
classes in this race during the Victorian and Edwardian
period. The practice sessions of each club would draw
crowds of hundreds and, occasionally, thousands so that
outings had to be re-scheduled for the very early morn-
ings. The race itself would bring out hundreds of
thousands to line the banks of the river for the whole
four-and-a-half mile course, and every bridge, as here,
would be crammed to overflowing. The huge convoy of
vessels which followed the crews can be seen above the
bridge at a distance considered safe by the umpires and
the Thames Conservancy.

78 Some superb Windermere class yachts pictured in 1887
during a race on the lake. The yachts were privately
owned by members of the Windermere Yacht Club and
in these races were helmed by expert sailing men, very
often Morecambe fishermen, brought up specially for the
occasion. Heavy bets were laid and the professionals
could be very well rewarded.

79 (*left*) As in all branches of competitive boating there existed in punting a split between amateurs and professionals. The amateurs were keen contenders but the professionals punted for a living and competed whenever they could for cash prizes. Abel Beesley, pictured here in 1887, was a full-time waterman in Oxford and first won the English championship in 1877 when he defeated E. Andrews in a match for £100. He remained unchallenged until 1886 when the professional championship was instituted at Maidenhead. He won this five years in succession before retiring in 1890.

80 (*above*) John Ritchie the assistant boatman to Berwick on Tweed Rowing Club making final adjustments to the club's new racing outrigger, in 1888. The boathouse by the bridge is that of Tweed R.C., a club formed for the town's artisans. It was quite common at this time to have two clubs next to each other, one for gentlemen and the other for players; they would rarely meet in competition.

81 The final of the English amateur punting champion-ship held on the River Thames at Shepperton in 1888. The racing punts used are quite unlike the touring punts of popular use, and their width is approximately the length of the punter's foot. They are ribbed in the state room for leverage, but because they were difficult to manoeuvre in a straight line the sport declined. Hap-pily, punting is enjoying a resurgence and the last women's champion is cur-rently director of coaching for the Amateur Rowing Association.

82 & 83 Both crews in the 1896 University Boat Race, Oxford on the River Thames at Putney and Cambridge on the River Cam. By 1896 the Boat Race had become a hugely popular mass spectator event and press coverage of the race and its preparation may be said to mark the beginning of sporting journalism. Never before had athletic contests, for instance, been written about so extensively. As the first of the mass spectator sports rowing was news. Punch magazine thought the Boat Race was thoroughly instructive as it showed annually that 'all was well with John Bull when pluck and gameness are so well exhibited' and concluded that 'There are worse schools than an eight oar with its discipline and training.' Oxford won by half a length!

84 The Worthing Rowing Club four at the 1898 regatta.
This event like many another was organized primarily to
furnish the local watermen and professionals with a
chance to augment their incomes. In each event, however, there would be races set aside for amateurs only,
and this photograph shows the crew from the Worthing
Amateur R.C. setting out for the senior race against the
amateur four from Brighton. They raced for one-and-a-
quarter miles passing under the pier twice.

85 The 1898 National Amateur Rowing Association
Regatta held from the West End ARA boathouse in
Hammersmith. This regatta was organized specially for
those clubs affiliated to NARA which were excluded
from wider competition by the ban on manual workers
imposed by the Amateur Rowing Association. The event
included crews from the docks, transport services, banks,
business and commercial institutions. The divisive 'manual' clause continued to give offence until the 1950s.

86 (*left*) Members of Ryde Rowing Club who rowed round the Isle of Wight in the then record time of ten-and-a-half hours. Such feats of endurance were popular and very much part of the boating scene, generally with marathon canoe trips made fashionable by 'Rob Roy' Macgregor in the years 1865-1872 and ocean sailing inaugurated by Joshua Slocum in 1895. The present record time for the Isle of Wight trip is eight hours and six minutes.

87 (*above*) The start of a canoe race in 1902; the exact location is unfortunately unknown but the subjects are of particular interest as they show the evolution of the type of boat very well. The canoe nearest the camera is a Canadian Canoe; the middle craft is an early Rob Roy style canoe, whilst the far boat is the later, more stream-lined edition of the Rob Roy in which John MacGregor completed his foreign trips. MacGregor was a rather eccentric ex-Varsity oarsman who raised money for his evangelical work by paddling his self-designed canoe along the rivers of Europe and then writing very popular books about his adventures. His books and canoe enjoyed a considerable vogue in the 1860s and 70s; the canoe was, of course, named after MacGregor's illustrious ancestor.

88 The Vesper Boat Club eight from Philadelphia on the water at Henley in 1905. The crew was tainted with professionalism since it was found, after their defeat by the Leander Club, that their trip to England had been subsidized by public subscription. The Henley Royal Regatta Committee banned the Vesper Boat Club and the members of the crew from further entry at the regatta. One member of the committee also tried to get all American crews banned, but failed.

89 Huntingdon Regatta in July 1906 featuring two Huntingdon Boat Club crews contesting the Junior Fours final. The event was held on early closing day, hence the huge crowds. The Boat Club headquarters can be seen on the right, adjacent to the boat hiring firm of Childs where organized rowing first started in the town during 1854.

90 The scene immediately following the final of Junior
Fours at the Agecroft regatta, Salford, in 1907. At this
point on the River Irwell the water is impounded by
Douglas Green Weir and this allows a three quarters of
a mile course, a fact which encouraged Agecroft R.C. to
move here in 1861. By the beginning of the twentieth
century, as the picture shows, industry was spreading
from the city centre. Today the area is engulfed by hous-
ing and industry.

91 A picture taken in 1907 of the motor launch *Satanella* on Lake Windermere with her owner Leonard Williamson on board. *Satanella* was built in this same year and exhibits the stream-lined design of a new series of power boats. She could attain a top speed of 23 mph and used 40 gallons of paraffin per hour in order to do so! She is seen here flying the pennant of Mersey Yacht Club.

92 Fleetwood .Regatta in 1907. There had been regattas for sailing and rowing on the River Wyre at Knott End since the 1830s, primarily amongst the local fishermen. When Sir Hesketh Fleetwood planned and developed the town the regatta became an important commercial attraction. The photograph shows the estuary looking towards the Knott End ferry terminus with a sailing race in progress and the Hesketh family schooner, dressed overall, acting as the committee boat.

93 (*above*) The tea interval at the Loe and Feock Regatta on the River Fal, in August 1909. Such regattas, being a combination of rowing, sailing and swimming events, were very popular at this time and drew large crowds from the inland towns. The sports finished with the contestants swimming under the committee boat seen with the bow flag on the far left of the picture.

94 (*right*) A gondola pictured during a tea interval on the course at Henley Royal Regatta, in July 1890. It was fashionable to be seen at this event and even more so if one could acquire an unusual craft in which to appear. This gondola was always much in demand, being the only one available, and was rented out by the local hiring firm who provided a suitably dressed gondolier – apart from the hat!

95 This picture, taken in 1895, shows just one of the uses to which the Berthon Collapsible Boat could be put. Edward Berthon was an Anglican clergyman who invented collapsible boats and canoes to meet the demand shown by the public following MacGregor's exploits in the 1860s and 70s. Constructed of canvas on wooden frames, they could be prepared for use in a few seconds, and one large enough to take half-a-dozen passengers could be carried on a pack saddle.

96 Tommy Rogers of Ironbridge on the River Severn, pictured here at the turn of the century, with one of many coracles he made at his workshop by the bridge. The coracles were officially used for cheap cross-river transport and licensed fishing, but were heavily employed at night for poaching rabbits in the riverside woods; they were also raced at local regattas for cash prizes. Tommy's grandson, Eustace, continues the family business today.

97 The Goring and Streatly Reagtta of 1902 on the
Thames showing the enclosure and winning post with
the final of the mixed punt paddling event about to end.
Punt paddling was known as dongola racing having been
named after the province of Sudan through which Kitch-
ener's troops paddled similar craft in the wars of 1898.
Many regattas finished their programmes with similar
novelty events in order to retain the lighter side of
increasingly serious competitive occasions. The marquee
on the right housed the inevitable Edwardian accompan-
iment of the military band.

98 Mr E. A. Rowell, a stalwart of the local rowing club, trying out his home-made water cycle on the River Ouse at St Neots in Cambridgeshire, with St Neot's mediaeval bridge in the background, sometime in 1910. Mr Rowell (an excellent name for an oarsman!) was the local tailor from New Street and was well known for his ingenuity and inventiveness, and the water cycle is a prime example of the Edwardian penchant for something different.

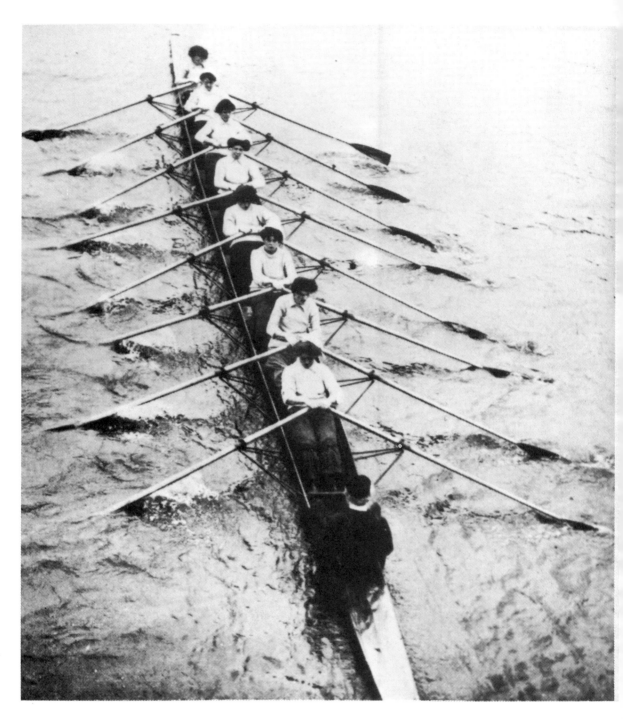

99 A rare picture of Frederick Furnivall coxing his octuple sculler; it was taken from Hammersmith Bridge in 1906. The crew is of London shop girls and they are off on a trip to Putney and back, although the real reason for the outing was to be photographed and written up in the press. The resulting publicity allowed Fred further scope for soliciting patronage for the girls' sculling club.

100 Frederick James Furnivall, a towering figure in the history of boating, pictured here on his eighty-fifth birthday in 1910 by the boathouse of the club he established for the working girls of London in Hammersmith. He had already formed the National Amateur Rowing Association to cater for those debarred from competing by the exclusive rules of the Amateur Rowing Association. After his death in 1911 his club became the Furnivall Sculling Club, a name it still retains.

Acknowledgements

The author would like to thank the following people and companies for their help in the compilation of this book:
The Local Studies Libraries of Shrewsbury, Lincoln, Wigan, Liverpool, Nottingham, Oxford, Salford, Huntingdon and Knaresborough; Documentary Photo Archive of Manchester; the Royal Photographic Society of Bath; the Steamboat Museum of Windermere; the Ironbridge Gorge Museum; the Northumberland Records Office; Pamlin Prints of Croydon; the Wyre Forest District Council Museum Service at Bewdley; Agecroft Rowing Club; Ryde Rowing Club; Nick Walmsley of Norwich Union R.C.; Richard du Parq of Cygnet R.C.; Bill Shufflebottom of Northwich R.C.; Robin Parkin of Berwick on Tweed R.C.; Raymond Mark of Talkin Tarn R.C.; Bill Collins of Stratford on Avon R.C.; Ralph Bird of Truro R.C.; Robert Elleray of Worthing Library and Ed Tyson, bookseller of Lancaster.